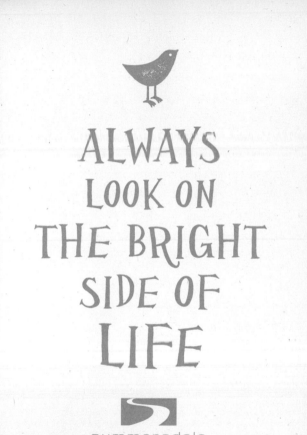

ALWAYS
LOOK ON
THE BRIGHT
SIDE OF
LIFE

summersdale

ALWAYS LOOK ON THE BRIGHT SIDE OF LIFE

Copyright © Summersdale Publishers Ltd, 2014

Research by Sarah Viner

Summersdale Publishers Ltd
46 West Street
Chichester
West Sussex
PO19 1RP
UK

www.summersdale.com

Printed and bound in the Czech Republic

ISBN: 978-1-84953-527-4

Substantial discounts on bulk quantities of Summersdale books are available to corporations, professional associations and other organisations. For details contact Nicky Douglas by telephone: +44 (0) 1243 756902, fax: +44 (0) 1243 786300 or email: nicky@summersdale.com.

TO...

FROM...

KEEP SMILING, BECAUSE
LIFE IS A BEAUTIFUL
THING AND THERE'S SO
MUCH TO SMILE ABOUT.

Marilyn Monroe

IT IS ALWAYS THE
SIMPLE THAT PRODUCES
THE MARVELLOUS.

Amelia Barr

MUDDY WATER, LET STAND, BECOMES CLEAR.

Lao Tzu

ENERGY AND PERSISTENCE CONQUER ALL THINGS.

Benjamin Franklin

THE BEST THING TO HOLD ON TO IN LIFE IS EACH OTHER.

Audrey Hepburn

THE MORE WE DO, THE MORE WE CAN DO.

William Hazlitt

LOOK ON EVERY EXIT
AS BEING AN ENTRANCE
SOMEWHERE ELSE.

Tom Stoppard

A SMILE IS A CURVE THAT SETS EVERYTHING STRAIGHT.

Phyllis Diller

EVERY DAY BRINGS
A CHANCE FOR YOU
TO DRAW IN A BREATH,
KICK OFF YOUR SHOES...
AND DANCE.

Oprah Winfrey

THE WAY I SEE IT,
IF YOU WANT THE
RAINBOW, YOU GOTTA
PUT UP WITH THE RAIN.

Dolly Parton

THIS LIFE IS NOT FOR COMPLAINT, BUT FOR SATISFACTION.

Henry David Thoreau

YOU CAN'T EXPECT
TO HIT THE JACKPOT
IF YOU DON'T PUT A
FEW NICKELS IN
THE MACHINE.

Flip Wilson

WHAT MAKES THE
DESERT BEAUTIFUL...
IS THAT SOMEWHERE
IT HIDES A WELL.

Antoine de Saint-Exupéry

IF YOU LOOK THE RIGHT
WAY, YOU CAN SEE THAT
THE WHOLE WORLD IS
A GARDEN.

Frances Hodgson Burnett

LIFE IS LIKE PHOTOGRAPHY; WE DEVELOP FROM THE NEGATIVES.

Anonymous

YOU ARE NEVER TOO
OLD TO SET ANOTHER
GOAL OR TO DREAM
A NEW DREAM.

C. S. Lewis

THERE IS NOTHING
IMPOSSIBLE TO HIM
WHO WILL TRY.

Alexander the Great

EXPECT PROBLEMS
AND EAT THEM
FOR BREAKFAST.

Alfred A. Montapert

THOSE WHO WISH TO SING ALWAYS FIND A SONG.

Swedish proverb

NOTHING IN THE
WORLD IS EVER
COMPLETELY WRONG.
EVEN A STOPPED CLOCK
IS RIGHT TWICE A DAY.

Paulo Coelho

I DON'T THINK OF
ALL THE MISERY, BUT
OF THE BEAUTY THAT
STILL REMAINS.

Anne Frank

FAILURES ARE LIKE
SKINNED KNEES:
PAINFUL BUT
SUPERFICIAL.

H. Ross Perot

IN THE MIDDLE OF DIFFICULTY LIES OPPORTUNITY.

Albert Einstein

DON'T GO THROUGH LIFE, GROW THROUGH LIFE.

Eric Butterworth

MIGHTY OAKS FROM LITTLE ACORNS GROW.

Anonymous

LAUGH AND THE WORLD LAUGHS WITH YOU.

Ella Wheeler Wilcox

WHEREVER YOU GO,
NO MATTER WHAT THE
WEATHER, ALWAYS
BRING YOUR OWN
SUNSHINE.

Anthony J. D'Angelo

ONE JOY
SCATTERS
A HUNDRED
GRIEFS.

Chinese proverb

ENTHUSIASM MOVES THE WORLD.

Arthur Balfour

IF YOU CAN'T GET RID OF
THE SKELETON IN YOUR
CLOSET, YOU'D BEST
TEACH IT TO DANCE.

George Bernard Shaw

NOTHING IS A WASTE OF
TIME IF YOU USE THE
EXPERIENCE WISELY.

Auguste Rodin

TO BE WITHOUT SOME OF
THE THINGS YOU WANT
IS AN INDISPENSABLE
PART OF HAPPINESS.

Bertrand Russell

IT DOES NOT
MATTER HOW SLOWLY
YOU GO AS LONG AS YOU
DO NOT STOP.

Confucius

LOOK AT EVERYTHING
AS THOUGH YOU WERE
SEEING IT FOR THE
FIRST OR LAST TIME.

Betty Smith

WHEN LIFE LOOKS LIKE
IT'S FALLING APART, IT
MAY JUST BE FALLING
IN PLACE.

Beverley Solomon

IF YOU GIVE PEOPLE A
CHANCE, THEY SHINE.

Billy Connolly

EVERY MOMENT
HAS ITS PLEASURES
AND ITS HOPE.

Jane Austen

LIFE ISN'T ABOUT
WAITING FOR THE STORM
TO PASS; IT'S ABOUT
LEARNING TO DANCE
IN THE RAIN.

Anonymous

THROW CAUTION TO THE WIND AND JUST DO IT.

Carrie Underwood

SOME PEOPLE
GRUMBLE THAT ROSES
HAVE THORNS; I AM
GRATEFUL THAT THORNS
HAVE ROSES.

Alphonse Karr

THE MAN WHO
REMOVES A MOUNTAIN
BEGINS BY CARRYING
AWAY SMALL STONES.

Chinese proverb

ALL THE STATISTICS
IN THE WORLD CAN'T
MEASURE THE WARMTH
OF A SMILE.

Chris Hart

HAPPINESS IS NOT AN IDEAL OF REASON, BUT IMAGINATION.

Immanuel Kant

YOU LIVE BUT ONCE; YOU MIGHT AS WELL BE AMUSING.

Coco Chanel

IF YOU THINK YOU
ARE TOO SMALL TO
MAKE A DIFFERENCE,
TRY SLEEPING WITH
A MOSQUITO.

Dalai Lama

THERE IS ALWAYS ROOM
AT THE TOP.

Daniel Webster

THE WORLD IS ALWAYS OPEN, WAITING TO BE DISCOVERED.

Dejan Stojanović

GIVE LIGHT, AND
THE DARKNESS WILL
DISAPPEAR OF ITSELF.

Desiderius Erasmus

WHEN ASKED IF MY
CUP IS HALF FULL OR
HALF EMPTY MY ONLY
RESPONSE IS THAT I AM
THANKFUL I HAVE A CUP.

Anonymous

LIFE SHRINKS OR EXPANDS IN PROPORTION TO ONE'S COURAGE.

Anaïs Nin

I MAY NOT HAVE GONE
WHERE I INTENDED TO
GO, BUT I THINK I HAVE
ENDED UP WHERE I
NEEDED TO BE.

Douglas Adams

THERE ARE TWO WAYS
OF SPREADING LIGHT:
TO BE THE CANDLE
OR THE MIRROR THAT
REFLECTS IT.

Edith Wharton

AMBITION CAN CREEP AS WELL AS SOAR.

Edmund Burke

BE GLAD OF LIFE
BECAUSE IT GIVES YOU
THE CHANCE TO LOVE, TO
WORK, TO PLAY AND TO
LOOK UP AT THE STARS.

Henry van Dyke

WITH THE NEW DAY COMES NEW STRENGTH AND NEW THOUGHTS.

Eleanor Roosevelt

THE SWEETEST
PLEASURES ARE THOSE
WHICH ARE HARDEST
TO BE WON.

Giacomo Casanova

PERSEVERANCE IS
FAILING NINETEEN
TIMES AND SUCCEEDING
THE TWENTIETH.

Julie Andrews

SOME DAYS THERE WON'T BE A SONG IN YOUR HEART. SING ANYWAY.

Emory Austin

YOU CAN'T MAKE AN OMELETTE WITHOUT BREAKING EGGS.

English proverb

PLUNGE BOLDLY INTO
THE THICK OF LIFE,
AND SEIZE IT WHERE
YOU WILL, IT IS ALWAYS
INTERESTING.

Johann Wolfgang von Goethe

NOTHING IS IMPOSSIBLE,
THE WORD ITSELF SAYS
'I'M POSSIBLE!'

Audrey Hepburn

START BY DOING WHAT'S
NECESSARY; THEN DO
WHAT'S POSSIBLE; AND
SUDDENLY YOU ARE
DOING THE IMPOSSIBLE.

Francis of Assisi

TURN YOUR FACE TO THE
SUN AND THE SHADOWS
FALL BEHIND YOU.

Maori proverb

POSITIVE ANYTHING
IS BETTER THAN
NEGATIVE NOTHING.

Elbert Hubbard

IT IS NEVER TOO LATE
TO BE WHAT YOU MIGHT
HAVE BEEN.

George Eliot

IF YOU CAN FIND A PATH
WITH NO OBSTACLES,
IT PROBABLY DOESN'T
LEAD ANYWHERE.

Frank A. Clark

FIND ECSTASY IN LIFE;
THE MERE SENSE OF
LIVING IS JOY ENOUGH.

Emily Dickinson

NO GREAT THING IS CREATED SUDDENLY.

Epictetus

AERODYNAMICALLY THE
BUMBLEBEE SHOULDN'T
BE ABLE TO FLY, BUT
THE BUMBLEBEE
DOESN'T KNOW SO IT
GOES FLYING ANYWAY.

Mary Kay Ash

WHY NOT JUST LIVE
IN THE MOMENT,
ESPECIALLY IF IT
HAS A GOOD BEAT?

Goldie Hawn

OPPORTUNITY DANCES
WITH THOSE WHO ARE
ALREADY ON THE
DANCE FLOOR.

H. Jackson Brown Jr

THE IMPORTANT
THING... IS NOT HOW
MANY YEARS IN YOUR
LIFE, BUT HOW MUCH
LIFE IN YOUR YEARS!

Edward Stieglitz

FALL SEVEN TIMES, STAND UP EIGHT.

Japanese proverb

A HAPPY LIFE CONSISTS
NOT IN THE ABSENCE,
BUT IN THE MASTERY
OF HARDSHIPS.

Helen Keller

IF YOU ASK ME
WHAT I CAME INTO
THIS LIFE TO DO, I WILL
TELL YOU: I CAME TO
LIVE OUT LOUD.

Émile Zola

IT'S NEVER TOO
LATE — NEVER TOO
LATE TO START OVER,
NEVER TOO LATE
TO BE HAPPY.

Jane Fonda

SMOOTH SEAS
DO NOT MAKE
SKILFUL SAILORS.

African proverb

I THINK, WHAT HAS THIS
DAY BROUGHT ME, AND
WHAT HAVE I GIVEN IT?

Henry Moore

ONE DOESN'T DISCOVER
NEW LANDS WITHOUT
CONSENTING TO LOSE
SIGHT OF THE SHORE
FOR A VERY LONG TIME.

André Gide

BAD TIMES HAVE
A SCIENTIFIC VALUE.
THESE ARE OCCASIONS
A GOOD LEARNER WOULD
NOT MISS.

Ralph Waldo Emerson

I DON'T MEASURE A
MAN'S SUCCESS BY HOW
HIGH HE CLIMBS BUT
HOW HIGH HE BOUNCES
WHEN HE HITS BOTTOM.

George S. Patton

EVERY LOT HAS
ENOUGH HAPPINESS
PROVIDED FOR IT.

Fyodor Dostoevsky

SINCE THE HOUSE
IS ON FIRE LET US
WARM OURSELVES.

Italian proverb

THE SUN IS NEW EACH DAY.

Heraclitus

MISTAKES ARE THE
PORTALS OF DISCOVERY.

James Joyce

WHOEVER IS HAPPY
WILL MAKE OTHERS
HAPPY TOO.

Anne Frank

IF THINGS ARE GOING
UNTOWARDLY ONE
MONTH, THEY ARE SURE
TO MEND THE NEXT.

Jane Austen

HE WHO HAS BEGUN
IS HALF DONE.

Horace

WHEN YOU REACH
THE END OF YOUR ROPE,
TIE A KNOT IN IT AND
HANG ON.

Thomas Jefferson

THE ROUGHEST ROAD
OFTEN LEADS TO THE TOP.

Christina Aguilera

I CAN'T CHANGE THE
DIRECTION OF THE WIND,
BUT I CAN ADJUST MY
SAILS TO ALWAYS REACH
MY DESTINATION.

Jimmy Dean

DARING IDEAS ARE
LIKE CHESSMEN MOVED
FORWARD. THEY MAY BE
BEATEN, BUT THEY MAY
START A WINNING GAME.

Johann Wolfgang von Goethe

IF WE HAD NO WINTER,
THE SPRING WOULD NOT
BE SO PLEASANT.

Anne Bradstreet

FEELINGS ARE
MUCH LIKE WAVES,
WE CAN'T STOP THEM
FROM COMING, BUT WE
CAN CHOOSE WHICH
ONES TO SURF.

Jonatan Mårtensson

LET YOUR HOOK
BE ALWAYS CAST; IN
THE POOL WHERE YOU
LEAST EXPECT IT, THERE
WILL BE FISH.

Ovid

MAY YOU LIVE
EVERY DAY OF
YOUR LIFE.

Jonathan Swift

THE ROBBED THAT
SMILES, STEALS
SOMETHING FROM
THE THIEF.

William Shakespeare

ISN'T IT NICE TO THINK
THAT TOMORROW IS
A NEW DAY WITH NO
MISTAKES IN IT YET?

L. M. Montgomery

DON'T GET YOUR KNICKERS IN A KNOT. NOTHING IS SOLVED AND IT JUST MAKES YOU WALK FUNNY.

Kathryn Carpenter

I CAN, THEREFORE
I AM.

Simone Weil

I'D RATHER REGRET THE
THINGS I'VE DONE THAN
REGRET THE THINGS I
HAVEN'T DONE.

Lucille Ball

IF YOU LEARN FROM
DEFEAT, YOU HAVEN'T
REALLY LOST.

Zig Ziglar

FOR EVERY MINUTE
YOU ARE ANGRY YOU
LOSE SIXTY SECONDS
OF HAPPINESS.

Ralph Waldo Emerson

NEVER LOOK BACKWARDS
OR YOU'LL FALL DOWN
THE STAIRS.

Rudyard Kipling

IF OPPORTUNITY DOESN'T
KNOCK, BUILD A DOOR.

Milton Berle

THERE ARE ALWAYS FLOWERS FOR THOSE WHO WANT TO SEE THEM.

Henri Matisse

YESTERDAY IS GONE.
TOMORROW HAS NOT YET
COME. WE HAVE ONLY
TODAY. LET US BEGIN.

Mother Teresa

HAPPINESS OFTEN
SNEAKS IN THROUGH A
DOOR YOU DIDN'T KNOW
YOU LEFT OPEN.

John Barrymore

OPPORTUNITY OFTEN
COMES DISGUISED IN THE
FORM OF MISFORTUNE,
OR TEMPORARY DEFEAT.

Napoleon Hill

YOU CAN'T TURN BACK THE CLOCK BUT YOU CAN WIND IT UP AGAIN.

Bonnie Prudden

WE ARE ALL IN
THE GUTTER BUT SOME
OF US ARE LOOKING AT
THE STARS.

Oscar Wilde

ALL GREAT ACHIEVEMENTS REQUIRE TIME.

Maya Angelou

OPPORTUNITIES MULTIPLY AS THEY ARE SEIZED.

Sun Tzu

YOU CAN CUT ALL THE
FLOWERS BUT YOU
CANNOT KEEP SPRING
FROM COMING.

Pablo Neruda

OUR BEST SUCCESSES
OFTEN COME AFTER
OUR GREATEST
DISAPPOINTMENTS.

Henry Ward Beecher

SOME DAYS YOU'RE THE
BUG. SOME DAYS YOU'RE
THE WINDSHIELD.

Price Cobb

THE SWEETEST
PLEASURE ARISES FROM
DIFFICULTIES OVERCOME.

Publilius Syrus

IT IS OFTEN IN
THE DARKEST SKIES
THAT WE SEE THE
BRIGHTEST STARS.

Richard Evans

IF YOU'RE ALREADY
WALKING ON THIN ICE,
YOU MIGHT AS
WELL DANCE.

Proverb

WHAT WE SEE DEPENDS MAINLY ON WHAT WE LOOK FOR.

John Lubbock

OPPORTUNITIES DON'T
OFTEN COME ALONG.
SO, WHEN THEY DO, YOU
HAVE TO GRAB THEM.

Audrey Hepburn

DON'T JUDGE EACH DAY
BY THE HARVEST YOU
REAP BUT BY THE SEEDS
THAT YOU PLANT.

Robert Louis Stevenson

THERE ARE NO TRAFFIC JAMS ALONG THE EXTRA MILE.

Roger Staubach

VICTORY BELONGS TO
THE MOST PERSEVERING.

Napoleon Bonaparte

DO NOT THINK OF
TODAY'S FAILURES, BUT
OF THE SUCCESS THAT
MAY COME TOMORROW.

Helen Keller

WHERE THERE IS RUIN,
THERE IS HOPE FOR
A TREASURE.

Rumi

THE AVERAGE PENCIL
IS SEVEN INCHES LONG,
WITH JUST A HALF-INCH
ERASER — IN CASE YOU
THOUGHT OPTIMISM
WAS DEAD.

Robert Brault

LIFE IS A SHIPWRECK,
BUT WE MUST NOT
FORGET TO SING IN
THE LIFEBOATS.

Voltaire

LIFE ISN'T ABOUT
FINDING YOURSELF.
LIFE IS ABOUT
CREATING YOURSELF.

George Bernard Shaw

EVEN BEES, THE
LITTLE ALMSMEN OF
SPRING BOWERS,
KNOW THERE IS
RICHEST JUICE IN
POISON-FLOWERS.

John Keats

WHO SEEKS
SHALL FIND.

Sophocles

EVERY MAN IS THE SMITH OF HIS OWN FORTUNE.

Swedish proverb

ONLY THOSE WHO WILL
RISK GOING TOO FAR CAN
POSSIBLY FIND OUT HOW
FAR ONE CAN GO.

T. S. Eliot

REGARD MISTAKES AS
TEACHERS, NOT JUDGES.

Tae Yun Kim

JUST BE YOURSELF, THERE IS NO ONE BETTER.

Taylor Swift

I'VE LEARNED THAT
WHEN YOU HARBOUR
BITTERNESS, HAPPINESS
WILL DOCK ELSEWHERE.

Andy Rooney

PERHAPS OUR EYES NEED
TO BE WASHED BY OUR
TEARS ONCE IN A WHILE,
SO THAT WE CAN SEE
LIFE WITH A CLEARER
VIEW AGAIN.

Alex Tan

IF WE ALL DID THE
THINGS WE ARE CAPABLE
OF, WE WOULD ASTOUND
OURSELVES.

Thomas Edison

ALWAYS LAUGH WHEN YOU CAN. IT IS CHEAP MEDICINE.

Lord Byron

THE LIMITS OF THE
POSSIBLE CAN ONLY
BE DEFINED BY GOING
BEYOND THEM INTO
THE IMPOSSIBLE.

Arthur C. Clarke

A SMILE IS A FACELIFT
THAT'S IN EVERYONE'S
PRICE RANGE.

Tom Wilson

EVERYTHING IS OK IN
THE END. IF IT'S NOT OK,
THEN IT'S NOT THE END.

Anonymous

LAUGH AS IF IT'S
FUNNY, EMBRACE AS
IF IT'S LOVE, AND
SMILE ANYWAY.

Richelle E. Goodrich

A GENTLE WORD, A
KIND LOOK, A GOOD-
NATURED SMILE CAN
WORK WONDERS AND
ACCOMPLISH MIRACLES.

William Hazlitt

ANGELS CAN FLY
BECAUSE THEY TAKE
THEMSELVES LIGHTLY.

G. K. Chesterton

ACT AS IF WHAT YOU DO
MAKES A DIFFERENCE.
IT DOES.

William James

HOW WONDERFUL IT
IS THAT NOBODY NEED
WAIT A SINGLE MOMENT
BEFORE STARTING TO
IMPROVE THE WORLD.

Anne Frank

FOR MYSELF I AM AN
OPTIMIST — IT DOES NOT
SEEM TO BE MUCH USE
BEING ANYTHING ELSE.

Winston Churchill

A TREE DOESN'T FALL
WITH ONE BLOW.

Yiddish proverb

IF YOU LOVE LIFE, LIFE
WILL LOVE YOU BACK.

Arthur Rubinstein

OUR GREATEST GLORY IS
NOT IN NEVER FALLING,
BUT IN RISING EVERY
TIME WE FALL.

Confucius

IT JUST WOULDN'T
BE A PICNIC WITHOUT
THE ANTS.

Anonymous

SHOOT FOR THE MOON.
EVEN IF YOU FAIL,
YOU'LL LAND AMONG
THE STARS.

Les Brown

NO ONE IS USELESS
IN THIS WORLD WHO
LIGHTENS THE BURDENS
OF ANOTHER.

Charles Dickens

THE BEST IS
YET TO DO.

William Shakespeare

MY SUN SETS
TO RISE AGAIN.

Robert Browning

@EsmeTheBird

If you're interested in finding out more about our books, find us on Facebook at **Summersdale Publishers** and follow us on Twitter at **@Summersdale**.

www.summersdale.com